The Porch

a play by Jack Neary

978-853-9620

jack@jacknearyonline.com

www.jacknearyonline.com

Copying of the script is not permitted. For performance availability and royalty information, please contact the playwright.

The Porch

In its various stages of development, THE PORCH was produced professionally by:

> The Lyric Stage Company of Boston
>
> The Stoneham Theatre, Stoneham, MA (cover photo)
>
> Ann Baker and New Century Theatre, Northampton, MA
>
> The Majestic Theatre, West Springfield, MA

In this developmental stage, THE PORCH featured these exceptional professional actors:

> Ellen Colton, Cheryl McMahon, Bobbie Steinbach, Richard Snee, John Davin, Marina Re, Sheriden Thomas, Barbara McEwen, Stuart Gamble, J. T. Waite, Andrew Dolan

Also, in this developmental stage, THE PORCH was produced by the following community theatres:

> Act One, Portsmouth, NH
>
> Winchester Little Theatre, Winchester, VA
>
> Actors, Inc., Lowell, MA
>
> The Hovey Plays, Waltham, MA

<u>**THE PORCH** TAKES PLACE ON LABOR DAY WEEKEND, 2004</u>

A MILL TOWN IN EASTERN MASSACHUSETTS

<u>**THE PLAY IS PRESENTED IN TWO ACTS**</u>

THE PORCH

Scene One

The front porch of an old house in a well-populated neighborhood of an eastern Massachusetts mill town. The porch is spacious and features three comfortable chairs, all facing the street. There is a small table between two of the chairs. There is a screen door leading into the house (with a full open wooden door inside the screen door). There are two windows looking out onto the porch, with curtains and blinds. The blinds are raised at the top of the show.

We can see part of the sidewalk in front of the house. On one side of the house, the sidewalk winds around the street corner, where a bus stop and a bench are located. On the other side of the house is the approach to the back yard.

It is mid-afternoon, the day before Labor Day, 2004. The day is bright and warm.

GERT sits in one of the chairs, poring over Bill Clinton's autobiography. She is skirting around the age of seventy, and is more than happy to speak her mind at all times. She wears a comfortable running suit in which she has never run in her life. At one point, she holds the book up to the sunlight to get a better look and to show us the cover. She opens the book to a random page near the end, and reads again, encountering a particularly jarring passage.

                    GERT
Holy Mother of God.
          (reads some more)
No wonder his arteries clogged.

> *Through the screen door comes MARJORIE, who is approximately Gert's age. She is more tastefully (though equally comfortably) dressed than Gert. She is a pleasant, intelligent, sane human being.*

                    MARJORIE
Who?

                    GERT
          (holds up book)
Him.

                    MARJORIE
          (with not a little disdain)
Oh. Him.

                    GERT
How's she doin' in there?

                    MARJORIE
Well, she said she was gonna do it and she's doin' it. I give her credit.

                    GERT
          (sloughing it off)
Oh, credit...He's been dead five years.

                    MARJORIE
Still, this is a big thing for her...havin' the cookout again. Labor Day. Without Tom.

                    GERT
          (into book again)
She got us to help.

                    MARJORIE
Yeah, you're a big help.

                    GERT
I'm takin' a break!

                    MARJORIE

From what?

>   *The screen door opens and ALMA appears.
>   She is also in the same age ballpark as Gert
>   and Marjorie. She may dress a little better than
>   both of them, but she, too, makes sure what
>   she's wearing is comfortable. She's a bit hard
>   of hearing and on the ingenuous side.*

                    ALMA

Well, the bacon's wrapped around the little scallops and they're in the fridge so we can take a break.
>   (sits in middle chair)

                    GERT
>   (to Marjorie)

See!

                    MARJORIE

You said everybody gets here tomorrow at noon?

                    ALMA

Around there, yeah.
>   (to Gert; indicates book)

What is it?

                    GERT

The book? The one on him.
>   (shows it to her)

                    ALMA
>   (similarly disdainful)

Oh. Him.

                    GERT
>   (to Marjorie)

You gonna sit or you gonna stand there till Labor Day, 2005?

                    MARJORIE
>   (as she sits)

I'll sit till Alma gives me somethin' else to do.

>   *Gert puts the book on the table. All three sit
>   comfortably and stare straight ahead. After a*

moment, Gert begins to laugh, with insidious joy.

GERT
(points forward)
He can't park there, you know.

ALMA
What?

GERT
He can't park there.

ALMA
Who?

GERT
Him. There. With the car. Sister Bernadetta'll be outa the convent before he gets outa the car. You watch. She don't want anybody parkin' in the school parkin' lot. Since they got the new lines drawn and all the new spaces so it's easy to park, she don't want anybody parkin' there.

ALMA
Why not?

GERT
It's like all her life she's been waitin' for her own parkin' lot or somethin'. She's 12, her mother says whatdya wanna be, she says a nun or a parking lot attendant. She's like Mussolini with the parkin' lot. Look. Here she comes.
(beat, as they watch)
Look at 'im. "Yes, Sister. Yes, Sister. Sorry, Sister." You'd think she was carryin' a gun.

ALMA
She has a gun?

GERT
(loud; directly to Alma)
No. You'd think she was.

ALMA
Who?

GERT
Bernadetta.

ALMA
(to Marjorie)
I didn't see a gun. Did you?

MARJORIE
(loud, so Alma gets the point)
It was a joke, Alma. Gert told you a joke.

ALMA
(chuckles)
Oh.
(beat, stops chuckling)
I guess I don't get it.

GERT
(looks to parking lot)
There he goes.

ALMA
(longer beat; then, to Gert)
What's his name? Mussolini?

GERT
Never mind about Mussolini.

MARJORIE
Alma, pass me that book, please?
(she does; to Gert)
You didn't buy this, I hope.

GERT
You kiddin' me? Lib'ry.

MARJORIE
(thumbing through)
Is it all in here? What he done?

GERT
I didn't get that far. I'm about two and a half inches from that part.

                    MARJORIE
It is a big book.

                    GERT
Well, you know what they say when you got a big book...

                    MARJORIE
                    (chuckling)
Oh, Gert...

                    ALMA
What? If you got a big book, what?

                    GERT
Then you got a big...
                    (prompts Alma)

                    ALMA
What?

                    MARJORIE
Never mind, Alma. Stop it, Gert.

                    ALMA
                    (thinking)
...When you got a big book...

                    MARJORIE
Alma! Forget it!
                    (thumbs book again)
So, can they put that in there? What he done?

                    GERT
Sure they can! They wanna sell the books, don't they?

                    MARJORIE
Well, I suppose they'd sell more books if they did.

                    ALMA
What?

                    MARJORIE
Put it in.

GERT
Puttin' it in's what he did best, from what I could tell.
(laughs)

MARJORIE
Gert!

GERT
Oh, look at the thing. The size of that book. Like we should pay good money to read about him. I remember him when it happened, him lookin' in the camera as if he was talkin' to me, sayin' them things to me like he knew me.

MARJORIE
He was a smoothy, all right.

GERT
Thinks I don't know he's full of it.

ALMA
(grabs and points to book)
Him?

MARJORIE
He's a politician.

ALMA
You know, they said he mighta did it with...uh...

GERT
Whatdya mean he mighta did it?

ALMA
With...that girl. The fat girl. With the funny hat.

GERT
There was no "mighta" about it!

MARJORIE
But the people still liked him.

ALMA
It was on the T.V.

MARJORIE
All the polls. They liked him.

ALMA
The Polacks liked him?

MARJORIE
A lot of people still like him.

GERT
I'll tell you who likes him. The people who do what he done like him because they done it too, and they wanna keep doin' it and it makes 'em feel better to know he done it and he got away with it.

MARJORIE
Slick Willy, they call him.

GERT
And those of us who only do it when we're supposed to do it, nobody asks us what <u>we</u> think.

MARJORIE
I wonder why.

GERT
Because them that take the polls wanna keep doin' it too. It's one of them conspiracies.

ALMA
I thought he said he didn't do it.

GERT
What?

ALMA
He said it on the T.V. "I did not have sexual...relations with that woman...Miss..." whatever her name is...the Polish girl.
    (to Marjorie)
Maybe that's why they like him.

GERT
Well...that's what he thought, you know.

MARJORIE
Well...

GERT
He thought what he done wasn't sexual relations.

ALMA
Wait a minute...

GERT
He thinks we're dumb enough to believe that what he done wasn't sexual relations in the "legal sense."

ALMA
Wait a minute. Did he or didn't he?

GERT
What?

ALMA
Do it.

GERT
Well, that's where it gets tricky.

MARJORIE
Depends on what you mean, Alma.

ALMA
What depends?

MARJORIE
Well, President Clinton thought..or at least he says he thought...that what he did...with the girl...wasn't sexual relations.

ALMA
Well what was it he did?

MARJORIE
He...wasn't clear on that.

ALMA
He didn't know?

MARJORIE
Well...

ALMA
How can he not know what it is? He was the President.

MARJORIE
It's not that he didn't know what it is. He just thought...that the way he...did it, didn't...add up to... what he calls...sexual relations.

ALMA
(beat)
The way he did it?

MARJORIE
Yes.

ALMA
The way he did it don't add up?

MARJORIE
Not to him.

ALMA
(beat)
Well, once you do it, you know you did it, don't you?

GERT
It's the <u>way</u> he done it makes him say it wasn't relations.

ALMA
What <u>way</u> did he do it?

MARJORIE
Well, I can't...

ALMA
What way?

MARJORIE
I really don't want to...

ALMA
What way did he do it?

Alma and Marjorie get into a little ad-lib argument. Alma wants an answer. Marjorie doesn't want to contribute. Gert breaks it up, abruptly.

GERT
He did the oral!

                        ALMA
The oral?

                        GERT
He said for it to be sexual relations you have to have it with
intercourse.
            (beat, to the inquiring Alma)
With the genitals on the genitals.

                        ALMA
With the what on the what?

                        GERT
The genitals on the genitals. He says it isn't sexual relations if it's oral
sex.

                        ALMA
What kind of sex?

                        GERT
Oral.

                        ALMA
Oral?

                        GERT
Oral. You know what oral means, don't you?

                        ALMA
Out loud?

                        GERT
No. Oral. Oral. With the mouth.

                        ALMA
            (beat)
What, he talks while he's doin' it? Big deal.
            (shrugs)

                        GERT
Let's put it this way, when he's gettin' it done, if anybody's doin' any
talkin', it's him.
            (laughs)

ALMA
(to Marjorie)
What's she talkin' about?

MARJORIE
It's a different kind of sex, Alma. Not the way we used to do it.

GERT
Don't tell me you never heard of oral sex?

ALMA
I never heard of sex at all till after my fourth kid. We didn't call it anything, we just went at it. By that time I only knew one way and it worked, so we didn't do it any more ways.
(beat)
Once he let me be on top so he could see the Super Bowl. So what is it? Oral sex.

GERT
(to Marjorie)
Tell her.

MARJORIE
I'm not telling her.

ALMA
(to Marjorie)
Did you ever do it?

MARJORIE
(beat)
No.

ALMA
(to Gert)
Did you?

GERT
I thought about it. I asked the priest in confession once if I could. He said he'd get back to me. Two days later he gets transferred to Africa. So I never tried it.

ALMA
So what is it?

GERT
Figure it out. Oral. Oral. The mouth.

ALMA
Yeah, so what?

GERT
(gestures elaborately, phrase by
phrase)
Oral. The mouth. Sex. Sex. Oral sex.
(punctuates her gesture)

ALMA
(beat)
Kissin'?

GERT
Not kissin'. Kissin' involves two noses in the same general vicinity. With the oral, you got your noses in two different counties.
(illustrates elaborately pointing in
two different directions)

ALMA
What are we talkin' about here, sex with your nose?

GERT
No. We're talkin' about the vicinities where the various noses end up when the sex is happening.

ALMA
(beat)
What?

GERT
Look, what's the nearest thing to your nose on your face?

ALMA
My little mustache thingy.

GERT
That you kiss with! The nearest thing to your nose on your face that you kiss with.

ALMA
Lips?

GERT
Lips. So with the oral you follow your nose and that's where the lips end up. Yours and his. In different places.

ALMA
What places?

GERT
Well...she goes down there...

MARJORIE
Good Lord...

ALMA
Down where?

GERT
There. There. The sexual area.
        (another physical illustration)

ALMA
His sexual area?
        (repeats the illustration)

GERT
She goes down there and she...she...services him.

ALMA
So wait a minute, if she's down there...in his sexual area...with her nose...

GERT
Yes?

ALMA
Don't that mean her own sexual area is way off the target?

GERT
This time, her nose is her general sexual area.

MARJORIE
Jesus, Mary and Joseph.

ALMA
She's not...She's not...

GERT

Oh, yes, she is.

ALMA

Her nose...and his...thing?

GERT

Forget about the nose, Alma! Expand your horizons!

ALMA

Lips?

GERT

Lips.

ALMA
(major disbelief)

Go on!

GERT
(again, the illustration)

Oral. The mouth. Sex. Sex. Oral sex.

ALMA
(beat)

What'll they think of next?
(to Marjorie)
You knew about this?

MARJORIE

I read about it.

ALMA
(to Gert)

How did you find out?

GERT

They had a very special Maury Povich.

ALMA
(beat)

Then what happens?

GERT
To what?

ALMA
When she starts nosin' around down there, what happens then?

GERT
Well, that's when you get into personal preference.

MARJORIE
Oh, I think they took care of personal preference about the time she put her nose into his sexual area.
           (a little reprise of the illustration)

GERT
Well, I mean once she's there, you know, with his whodjie in her...whatever...then it's up to them, you know, to decide how far they want to go.

ALMA
You're not tellin' me...

GERT
I'm not tellin' you anything except that if you're on the receivin' end of that particular main course, you better decide pretty quick whether or not you want dessert.

MARJORIE
        (disgusted)
Oh, Gert...

GERT
I'm just sayin'...

ALMA
Dessert?

MARJORIE
        (to Gert)
Don't look at me.

GERT
So, you can imagine. Either you want to deal with it or you don't. If you don't, you gotta be very agile with your neck.
           (illustrates, graphically)

ALMA
(long beat)
So that's what he was doin' with the Polish girl out in the hallway.

GERT
Seems to be. He just didn't think it counted as relations, though.
    (looks out)
Look! She got another one!

MARJORIE
Why doesn't she just put up a couple of those orange cones, block off the entrance?

GERT
She likes catchin' them too much. It's a nun thing. The only way she'd be happier is if she could hit them with a fifty cent fine.

    LEO walks on to the porch from the street. He's a bantam-like little guy around seventy. He is Gert's husband. He heads directly for the front door, with very little acknowledgement of the ladies.

LEO
(to Marjorie, indicating door)
He back there?

MARJORIE
Who, Pat? Yeah, he's almost through settin' up the grill.
    (Leo moves to the door; Marjorie
      stops him)
Leo...Aren't you gonna say hello to your wife?

LEO
Why?

MARJORIE
She's your wife.

LEO
Which means I see her every day of my life. We're way past hello.
    (to Gert)
Ain't that right?

GERT
It's on a long list of things we're way past.

LEO
(to Marjorie)
See? I come all the way over here, I get insulted.

GERT
Tomorrow I'll make it easy for you. We'll stay home. I'll insult you there.

LEO
(cheerfully)
Hello, Sweetheart!

GERT
(cheerfully)
Hello, Dumplin'!

LEO
(drops cheer; to Marjorie)
Can I go in now?

MARJORIE
Oh, you two...

Leo goes inside. The ladies sit and stare forward again.

ALMA
(long beat, as they stare)
Oral sex.

MARJORIE
Times have changed, Alma.

ALMA
(beat, using Gert's illustration)
Oral. The mouth. Sex. Sex. Oral sex.
(Gert and Marjorie help her to remember to punctuate the illustration)

                    GERT
We should sic Bernadetta on Clinton. He wouldn't pull any of that stuff with her. Or at least she'd hit him for more than fifty cents.
                    (chuckles)

                    MARJORIE
Oh, Gert...

                    ALMA
Oral sex.
                    (gets up, goes to door, opens it,
                     stops, turns...)
I won't sleep for a month.
                    (goes inside)

                    Blackout

                    Scene Two

                    A bit later in the afternoon. Leo now sits in Gert's chair, reading the Clinton book. He looks up, checks that no one is around, and skips to the later pages. PAT enters from the house. He is in the same age range as the others, and is Marjorie's husband. He's lankier than Leo, and a solid citizen. He carries a note pad and a stack of cards. He acknowledges Leo's reading as he takes a seat in Marjorie's chair.

                    PAT
Whatcha got there?
                    (Leo holds up book)
Oh. Him.

                    LEO
It's amazin' he got away with that stuff.

                    PAT
Oh, yeah. With the girl.

                    LEO
Guys like him get away with everything. If he's a Republican, he don't get away with it.

PAT
If he's a Republican, he don't know how to do it.

LEO
If I did somethin' like that and Gert found out...

PAT
What? She'd leave you?

LEO
Worse. I'd never get my hands on the clicker again.
(gestures using the remote)

PAT
(sits, hands notepad to Leo)
Here.

LEO
What?

PAT
(almost reciting)
You gotta read me the names there and I gotta write the names on these cards here with this red Magic Marker.
(which he produces)
Some kinda game for the kids tomorrow. Every kid gets a card. I don't know. I do what they tell me.

LEO
You can't read the names yourself?

PAT
I forgot my glasses. Read.

LEO
Jesus.
(takes out his own glasses, reads)
Kimberly. With a "K."

PAT
(beat)
Whatdya think, I was gonna start with a "Q?"
(writes; Leo waits)

LEO
You done?

PAT
Quiet. I'm bein' artistic.
(writes)
So... She's askin'.

LEO
Who?

PAT
Marjorie.

LEO
What, the trip?

PAT
You goin'?

LEO
(dismissing it)
Another bus?

PAT
She's askin'.

LEO
Where to?

PAT
The North Shore. The Music Theatre.

LEO
For what?

PAT
Lawrence Welk.

LEO
Lawrence Welk is dead.

PAT
The ones that ain't dead.

LEO
Some of 'em ain't dead?

PAT
There's a whole raft of 'em refuse to die. Another name.

LEO
Ashley.

PAT
(facetiously)
With an A?
(writes)

LEO
I hate the trips.

PAT
I know you hate the trips.

LEO
Forty-two widows and six guys that can't take a leak in less than twenty minutes.

PAT
She makes me ask, I ask.

LEO
Last year, there, remember we went to the Melody Tent to see...who was it?

PAT
Engle...dingle...

LEO
Bingle...dingle...dinkle...

PAT
Humperdink!

LEO
Right! Him! And he did the requests...Gert with the song.

PAT
Your song. You danced up on the stage. It was lovely.

LEO
It was embarrassing.

PAT
What was that song? Your song?

LEO
"Only You."

PAT
"Only You!" Yes!

LEO
He didn't even sing it right. Engle dinkle.

PAT
It was lovely.

LEO
I hate the trips.

PAT
(indicates list)
Gimme...

LEO
(reads)
Heather...Actually two Heathers.
(beat)
Jesus, what ever happened to "Mary" and "Katherine" and "Betty?"

PAT
They'll be on the trip.
(chuckles)

LEO
(beat, to Pat)
So you're goin'?

PAT
I got a choice?

LEO
Sure you got a choice. You're a man, right? Make your choice. Tell her your choice. Choose your choice and stick to it.

PAT
I let her choose my choice. It's quieter. Come on. You go too.

LEO
I don't know. An hour and a half on a bus to see a show fulla people livin' off a dead accordion player.

PAT
Come on.

LEO
Where we eatin'?

PAT
The King's Grant. Off 128.

LEO
Chicken or fish, right?

PAT
Pick one.

LEO
Why is it always pick chicken or pick fish?

PAT
'Cause that's what it is.

LEO
I pick steak.

PAT
I'll tell her chicken.

LEO
Who says I'm goin'?

PAT
You're goin'. I'm goin'. And Frank and Tony and Gerard will be goin'.

LEO
(with a little attitude)
Gerard. Gerard loves the trips.

PAT
Leave Gerard alone.

LEO
No problem. I just want to make sure Gerard leaves me alone.

PAT
Oh, he's not like that.

LEO
No. You're right. He's not like that. Seventy-two years old, never married, lives with his two spinster sisters and a cat named Mathis. He's a regular John Wayne.

PAT
Good. You're goin'. Name.

LEO
(reads)
Nicole.
(beat)
Where're we meetin'?

PAT
(writes)
For the bus?
(points)
The school parkin' lot.

LEO
Are you kiddin' me? Where are people gonna leave their cars?

PAT
Right there, in the lot!

LEO
In the lot? With Bernadetta lurkin' ready to pounce?

PAT
She don't lurk.

LEO
She got a foldin' chair set up behind the grotto of the Blessed Mother.

PAT
Gimme a break.

LEO
You watch. We get back from Lawrence Welk, she'll have Magic Marker all over the windshields...

PAT
Come on...

LEO
(mimes writing)
"You have parked in Hell."
(underlines twice)

Gert appears at the screen door, chomping on a carrot.

GERT
How you comin' with the names?

PAT
Gettin' there.

GERT
Alma's lookin' for the cards.

PAT
I'm bein' artistic.

GERT
Oh. Well, here's a good idea...

PAT
What?

GERT
Don't be artistic. Get 'em done.
(bites the carrot, she leaves)

PAT
Nice she's in her Donna Reed mood as usual.

LEO

She's mad at me.

PAT

Why?

LEO
(Pat knows)
Why. Why do you think why?

PAT

Oh.

LEO

Oh, is right.

PAT

You're still...
(indicates Leo's lower half)

LEO

Still...

PAT

With the uh...

LEO

Still...

PAT

The floppy disk.

LEO

I'm at a loss.

PAT

Well...you know...

LEO

Never. In my whole life, this has never been a problem. Even after swimmin'. Never.

PAT

The old professor's takin' a sabbatical, huh?

LEO
Forty-two years, I'm married. Forty-two years, I give an order...BANG! He's standin' at attention!

PAT
The old mailman can't deliver the package, huh?

LEO
Gert's ready to murder me.

PAT
The old quarterback...

LEO
Will you knock it off, already!

PAT
(beat, then fast)
...can't scramble out of the pocket.

LEO
So it's funny to you.

PAT
Big deal. You're in a slump.
(points to Leo's list)

LEO
Shut up. Jennifer.

PAT
A little down period.
(writes)

LEO
Hey, I'm tellin' ya, if somethin' don't rise to the occasion pretty soon, my marriage is gonna be in trouble.

PAT
If your marriage wasn't in trouble, then I'd say your marriage was in trouble.

LEO
The comedian.

PAT
Leo. Relax. You're thinkin' about it too much.

LEO
She wants me to take the medicine.

PAT
What medicine?

LEO
That...new medicine they got. For this. The...what is it? The Niagara.

PAT
Viagra.

LEO
Bob Dole takes it, she tells me. I tell her good, go sleep with Bob Dole.

PAT
They got more than that now, you know. With the Viagra, they got the Levitra and they got the Cialis...

LEO
Why don't you put them names on a couple of cards. I'm sure they're on this list.

PAT
Funny. Gimme another one.

LEO
(from list)
Bethany.
(beat, as Pat writes)
I got a prescription, to shut her up. She ordered some. She put it on top of the VCR. Like there I can't miss it.

PAT
Clever.

LEO
Tuesday, Father McCarty comes over, collectin' for the annual food fund, sees it up there, gives me a look.

PAT

What kinda look?

LEO

You know, like...
(demonstrates look)
...like "Whatsa matter, Leo? I don't even use mine and I can get stiff in thirty seconds."

PAT

Don't pay any attention to him.

LEO
(looks below)
The little engine that couldn't.

PAT

Don't let it get you down.
(Leo reacts)
I mean--don't let it bother you so much.

LEO

Hey, when somethin' bothers you, it bothers you. You don't have control over the how much botherin'. I mean, I know what this means...

PAT

What does it mean?

LEO

It means the credits are rollin' is what it means. It means the library card's expirin' and there ain't gonna be any renewal.

PAT

Depends.

LEO

Well, yeah, eventually.

PAT
(beat)
No. I mean it depends. This is a time of life how it goes for you depends on how you treat it.

LEO
What's to treat it? It's breakin' down, I should give it a treat?

PAT
Give it a chance! Give yourself a chance! You got a condition, they got a medicine. Take the medicine. Fix the condition. Renew your library card. Name.

LEO
(from list)
Mandy.

PAT
Randy?

LEO
Mandy. Mmm.
(thinks)
I don't know.

PAT
Whatyda mean, you don't know?

LEO
I wanna try a couple other things first.

PAT
Like what?

LEO
Somethin' to give me a jump start, you know? Somethin' that ain't medicine.

PAT
Like what?

LEO
I don't know. Haven't you ever...tried somethin' to get the battery charged?

PAT
Never had to.

LEO
Never? Not once you had to dig down deep to trigger the mechanism?

PAT
Always been like the Globe in the morning to me.

LEO
The Globe? The newspaper?

PAT
Wake up. Open the door. There it is.
(beat)
Next.

LEO
(from list)
Hannah. Last one.
(beat; Pat writes)
You're lucky. I gotta get some stimulation.

PAT
Gert's not gettin' it done?

LEO
It's worse than that. She's so pissed off now, even when it starts to tingle a little bit, she gives me one of them looks, scares the poor little bastard back into hibernation.

PAT
So think of somebody else.

LEO
Yeah?

PAT
Sure. Turn the lights off. Assume the position. Think of somebody else.

LEO
Hmm.

PAT
Who does it for you?

LEO
Really? You want me to tell you?

PAT
Absolutely. Who do you think would get the old captain back up on the poop deck?

LEO
Well...you know...it's a little...wild...but I kinda like...that, uh...

PAT
Yeah? Who?

LEO
That, uh...Lara Flynn Boyle.

PAT
Who the hell is Lara Flynn Boyle?

LEO
She used to be on the TV. That lawyer show on Sunday nights.

PAT
THE PRACTICE?

LEO
Yeah.

PAT
Which one was she?

LEO
I don't know...the one who always gave 'em trouble. The prosecutor.

PAT
The prosecutor!

LEO
Yeah. I like her.

PAT
Are you shittin' me? I thought you'd come up with Betty White or Jackie Kennedy or somethin'. The prosecutor? What do you want to do, give yourself a coronary?

LEO
I'm tellin' ya, I got a big job to get done here!

PAT
But...Flora Lynn...

LEO
Lara Flynn...

PAT
Whatever her name is...you gotta be more careful, Leo. You gotta keep your fantasies on the bottom shelf where you can reach 'em.

LEO
You're a big help.

PAT
Take the medicine.

LEO
Hey, it's not magic, you know. Says right on the package it don't work unless you get yourself sexually excited. So I can't just "take the medicine." Unless I think about Lara Flynn Boyle at the same time, I might as well suck on a Rolaids.

PAT
Are there any side effects to the Viagra?

LEO
A couple. No big deal.

PAT
Like what?

LEO
Headache. Upset stomach. Facial flushes. Same as what I get when I eat Gert's meatloaf.

PAT
So give it a shot!

LEO
I don't know...

PAT
Come on! What have you got to lose?

LEO
Well, you know I...read one more thing on the package.

PAT
What?

LEO
Says it improves erections in four out of five guys.

PAT
So?

LEO
So...what if...I'm the fifth guy?

PAT
There's only one way to find out, buddy.

LEO
I know.

PAT
Be brave.

LEO
You're right.

PAT
Let's bring these in.

Pat rises, heads to door, Leo rises and follows.

LEO
I'll stop by the drug store later. Check out the magazine rack.

PAT
Lara Flynn Boyle?

LEO
She's on a lot of covers.

PAT
You be careful, my friend.

LEO
It's a risk I gotta take.

                    PAT
              (opens door, stops)
Leo?

                    LEO
              (as they stop)
Yeah?

                    PAT
Godspeed.

                    LEO
              (beat)
Oh, I don't need that.

                    PAT
What?

                    LEO
They say it lasts up to four hours.

                    PAT
It will. You won't. Come on.

              They enter the house.

              <u>Blackout</u>

              Scene Three

              A bit later on the same day. Gert and Marjorie are in their chairs. Gert is back at the Clinton book. Marjorie is looking at a newspaper.

                    MARJORIE
You sure she doesn't need us?

                    GERT
She snapped at me. "On the porch!" she said.

                    MARJORIE
She's gettin' a little antsy.

                    GERT
Antsy? Ha! Looney is more like it.

MARJORIE
Oh, stop...looney...

GERT
I'm just sayin'...

MARJORIE
Well, it's a hard day. Gettin' ready for it all. Without Tom.

GERT
It's more than that with her. I don't know.

MARJORIE
Yeah?

GERT
Yeah. Somethin'...

MARJORIE
Well, this time of year. The birthday.

GERT
Yeah. The birthday.

MARJORIE
She's puttin' herself through a lot today.
    (beat)
Tom.
    (beat)
The birthday.

GERT
    (whispers)
She's comin'!

Alma enters from the house, wiping her hands on her apron.

ALMA
Why don't we ever go to Bingo?

GERT
What?

ALMA

You see all the cars in the church parking lot on Tuesday? All of them at Bingo? There must be something good to it. Why don't we go?

GERT

Because it's for the seniors.

ALMA
(beat)

Oh.
(sits)

MARJORIE
(reading paper)

They're goin' ahead with the center. Says here.

GERT
(also reading newspaper)

'Course they're goin' ahead with the center. You got a group like that screamin' and yellin' for somethin', they're gonna get it. God forbid anybody says no to a group like that.

ALMA

What group?

GERT

The Gays and Lesbians.

ALMA

Oh. Them.

GERT

What? What do you mean, "them?"

ALMA

I mean them. There's them and there's us.

GERT

Where do you get off callin' them them and us us?

ALMA

Well...what they do...makes them them. What we do makes us us.

MARJORIE
Well, they say, you know, that...what they do...you know...is just as normal as what we do.

ALMA
Well, that's not sayin' much.

GERT
Yeah. According to them, what they do is...genetical.

ALMA
What?

GERT
Genetical.

ALMA
What does that mean?

GERT
It means they can't help it.

ALMA
Can't help what?

GERT
Doin' what they do.

MARJORIE
Well, it's not that they can't help it. It's more like they want to do it.
 (chuckling, to Gert)
You remember?

GERT
 (also chuckling)
I remember.

ALMA
Shut up, the both of you.

GERT
 (to Alma)
You thought...

MARJORIE
(laughing)
I nearly died laughin'...

Gert and Marjorie really enjoy laughing at this recollection.

GERT
(to Alma)
You remember?

ALMA
Shut up.

GERT
You thought they were homeless sexuals!

MARJORIE
Homeless sexuals!

ALMA
Well, that's what it sounded like.

GERT
You thought all these people got together and had sex but didn't have anyplace to live!

ALMA
Well, on the radio, that's what it sounded like.

MARJORIE
She was gonna open up her cellar, remember?

GERT
Throw down a couple of sleeping bags, give 'em a box lunch, let 'em go at it.

MARJORIE
Homeless sexuals!

ALMA
I was young. What did I know?

MARJORIE
You were fifty-six!

GERT
Oh, Alma, what would we do without you?

ALMA
Good question.

MARJORIE
Oh, yes!

ALMA
No, I mean it. That's a good question. What would you do without me? What would any of us do without the other ones?
(no response)
It could happen, you know.
(nothing)
It's out there, you know. Starin' us right in the face.

GERT
What is?

ALMA
Death.

GERT
(beat)
You have a tumor or somethin'?

ALMA
No, I don't have a tumor or nothin'. I just been thinkin' about it, is all. It ain't like if I don't think about it it ain't gonna happen.
(beat)
I signed up already.

GERT
For what?

ALMA
For the pre-burial. Down at McCabe's.

GERT
Pre-burial?

MARJORIE
That's smart, Alma. That's a smart thing to do. Pat and me signed up, too. Couple of years ago.

GERT
What is it? Pre-burial?

MARJORIE
Well, it's...you know...you go down to McCabe's and you...you know...you make plans.

GERT
Plans to what?

ALMA
To die.

GERT
I got no plans to die.

ALMA
Well, you should go to McCabe's then. They talk you right through it...

GERT
No! I mean I got no--plans--to die. Dyin' ain't somethin' I'm plannin' to do.

ALMA
Well, they had a special, so I signed up.

MARJORIE
(a little disappointed she missed it)
They had a special?

ALMA
Yeah. For a limited time only, you got a $3500 casket for $2750, plus they throw in extra flowers and the artist of your choice for the music at the wake.

MARJORIE
Music? We didn't sign up for the music.

ALMA
On the speaker. The artist of your choice. Part of the deal.

MARJORIE
Well...who did you choose?

ALMA
Mitch Miller.

GERT
Mitch Miller!

ALMA
Yeah. I like Mitch Miller.

GERT
Jesus God Almighty, you're gonna have Mitch Miller on the speaker at your wake?

ALMA
Yeah! Maybe everybody'll sing along!
(to Marjorie)
Who would you have?

MARJORIE
For wake music?

ALMA
Yeah.

MARJORIE
I don't know. Jerry Vale?

ALMA
He'd be good.
(to Gert)
You?

GERT
I'm not dyin'!

ALMA
Yeah, I know you're not dyin'. But if you did, who?

GERT
(beat; considers)
Herb Alpert and the Tijuana Brass.

ALMA
Go on!

GERT
Much bigger than Mitch Miller.

MARJORIE
Jerry Vale was pretty big.

GERT
Oh, Jerry Vale sings like a girl.

MARJORIE
Well, then, you better go first, because I'm havin' Jerry Vale.

GERT
I'm not goin' anywhere.

ALMA
Be prepared!

GERT
You sure you don't have a tumor?

ALMA
I don't have a tumor!

Leo and Pat enter from the house. As usual, Leo has limited interest in the ladies, and bounds down the stairs as he speaks.

LEO
Okay, the awning is up.

GERT
Did you put the table?

LEO
We put the table. It's ready to go.

GERT
Where you goin'?

LEO
We're gonna take a walk down the Elks.

GERT
(to Pat)
You too?

                    PAT
                (to Marjorie)
Me too?

                    MARJORIE
Go ahead.

                    ALMA
Thanks, boys.

                    PAT
No problem.

                    GERT
                (to Leo)
I want you home before nine.

                    LEO
Fine.

                    GERT
And I want you walkin' straight.
                (to Pat)
I want him walkin' straight.

                    PAT
No problem.
                (to Leo)
Go.

                    LEO
                (as they walk away)
Any more rules from anybody?

                    PAT
Go!

                Pat takes Leo by the shoulder and they walk away.

                    GERT
                (takes Clinton book, refers to Alma)
Mitch Miller.

MARJORIE
(taps Alma on the leg)
So, honey, how you doin'?

ALMA
Good. Doin' good.

MARJORIE
You're brave, you know. This is brave, what you're doin'.

ALMA
Oh, it ain't brave. It's just time.

MARJORIE
Yeah.

ALMA
Time to get it goin' again. The family missed it.

MARJORIE
It'll be nice for you to see the grandkids all together.

GERT
Nice and noisy.

MARJORIE
But nice.

ALMA
Yeah.
(beat; considers)
Time to get goin' again.

MARJORIE
Yeah.

ALMA
For a lot of things...

Gert looks up from the book. She and Marjorie catch eyes.

ALMA (cont'd)
I'm goin' in for a minute...
  (rises)

MARJORIE
You want us to...
  (also starts to rise)

ALMA
  (surprisingly agitated)
No. No...just a minute...I'll be back...just a minute...

Alms goes brusquely inside, then slaps down the blinds in both windows, shutting out the porch, and the ladies.

GERT
See what I mean? Looney.

Gert and Marjorie look at each other.

<u>*LIGHTS fade to black.*</u>

Scene Four

Hours later. Night. Leo and Pat enter near the bench at the bus stop. Leo is not walking all that straight.

PAT
  (indicates bench)
Sit here.

LEO
What?

PAT
It's ten-thirty. You already blew the curfew. You gotta at least walk straight. Sit here a bit.

LEO
Okay...okay...where was I with my story?

PAT
  (clearly sick of the story)
Oh, Jesus, the story...

LEO
Yeah! The story! Where was I?

PAT
You were at Foxwoods.

LEO
I'm tellin' ya somethin' now, I never told nobody before. I'm tellin' ya somethin' if she finds out, call the morgue, look for the toe tag with my name on it.

PAT
I'm waitin' here. You're at Foxwoods. My breath is bated.

LEO
I'm at the Blackjack table.

PAT
This was last Valentine's, you said. When we took the bus.

LEO
Right. The overnight on the bus to Foxwoods.

PAT
And you're at the Blackjack table.

LEO
I'm gettin' killed like I always do. She's with the slots. She don't care where I am.

PAT
Gert.

LEO
I'm gettin' low on cash. My ass feels like I'm sittin' on a pile a' drill bits. I'm thinkin' of packin' it in. So I start to yawn, but this one sittin' next to me...

PAT
The redhead with the low cut.

LEO
Low as it gets. She puts her hand on my arm and she says, "Oh, Leo. Just a little longer."

PAT

The redhead touched you?

LEO

She touched me. And she called me Leo.

PAT

That's your name.

LEO

It ain't tattooed on my forehead! She been payin' attention.

PAT

Okay.

LEO

So I says no, no I gotta go and she grabs my arm and...you know...cuddles up to me...snug...real snug....

PAT

So what'd you do?

LEO (cont'd)

What could I do?

PAT

Well, you coulda stood up, said goodnight, walked away, went to...

LEO

I stayed.

PAT

I figured.

LEO

And I started winnin'.

PAT

The Blackjack.

LEO

She keeps her hand on my arm. Before you know it, I break even, and a little more. So I says I'm gonna quit while I'm ahead.

PAT

What about Red?

LEO
She says "Good idea. Let's have a drink."

PAT
You're shittin' me.

LEO
(raises hand to swear)
May I burn in Hell.

PAT
Where was I durin' all this?

LEO
Steve and Edyie.

PAT
They're very talented.

LEO
They are.

PAT
So what'd you say?

LEO
To the drink?

PAT
Yeah.

LEO
No.

PAT
I figured.

LEO
Well, I said no, but it wasn't like a flat out no. Not like a no I won't do it. It was more like a no I could do it if I wanted to do it but no I'm not gonna do it and that's the way it is. That kinda no.

PAT
So you told her you were married.
(beat; no response)
Leo?

                    LEO
No.

                    PAT
No?

                    LEO
Not exactly.

                    PAT
Well, what did you tell her exactly?

                    LEO
I didn't tell her anything exactly. I went with the flow.

                    PAT
What flow?

                    LEO
The flow! There was flow! I hadn't had flow in years, so there it was and I went with it.

                    PAT
So where did you flow to?

                    LEO
Don't rush me.

                    PAT
Fine.

                    LEO
So I says to her I can't have a drink. She says okay, how about a walk? I says I can't. So she starts to giggle...kinda, you know, like...
          (he giggles)
...and when she giggles with the low cut, I'm tellin ya...

                    PAT
You don't have to tell me.

                    LEO
That dress...

PAT

All right...

LEO

Keepin' those things in...

PAT

I got it.

LEO

Nothin' short of heroic.

PAT

Tell your story!

LEO

Well...anyway...she says, "You can't drink. You can't walk. Is there anything you can do?"

PAT

You sure you wanna be tellin' me this?

LEO

It's you or the priest.

PAT

Go.

LEO

So I says, yeah, there's plenty I can do--what do you have in mind?

PAT

You said that?

LEO
(enjoying this)
I was feelin' reckless!

PAT

So what'd she say?

LEO

Well...she points at this...
(indicates his wedding ring)

PAT

Yeah?

LEO

And she says, "Livin'?" Meanin' Gert.

PAT

Yeah.

LEO

And I says, "Depends on what you mean by livin'."

PAT

You dog.

LEO

Reckless!

PAT

Playin' her like a harmonica.

LEO

So she says, "By living, I mean is the person attached to that ring somewhere on the premises?"

PAT

Jesus H. Christ.

LEO

What's the "H" mean in that?

PAT

I dunno. "Holy," maybe.

LEO

Anyway, this...this is the moment of truth. The redhead's lookin' at me like I ain't been looked at in years. And I mean...this is one gorgeous woman, Pat. We're talkin' a face like a movie star and a body like she hit sixty and ordered up a fresh one from high school. Absolutely delectable. And she's askin' me...

PAT

Yeah?

LEO

Me. A retired firefighter...

                    PAT
Who cares?

                    LEO
She's askin' me...if I wanna...

                    PAT
Yeah?

                    LEO
You know...do it.

                    PAT
You don't think she was just lookin' for a friend?

                    LEO
          (with a gesture)
There was nothin' friendly about them maracas, Patty, boy! She was lookin' for some action.

                    PAT
Next year I'm skippin' Steve and Edyie.

                    LEO
They're very talented.

                    PAT
They are.

                    LEO
So she says, "Well?" Askin' about the ring. So...I took a long, deep breath...and I give her two words.

                    PAT
"Happily married?"

                    LEO
"Recently deceased."

                    PAT
What???

                    LEO
I told ya! Reckless!

PAT
Reckless is one thing. Suicidal is somethin' else entirely.

LEO
So she reaches into her pocketbook and takes out a business card. She writes her room number on the back and she gives it to me. She walks to the elevator.

PAT
Tell me you didn't follow her to her room.

LEO
No. Are you nuts?

PAT
Thank God.

LEO
I took a shower first.

PAT
What?

LEO
Blackjack gives me the sweats, you know that! I couldn't go up to her room smellin' like that!

PAT
You went up to her room?

LEO
You breathe a word of this to Gert, so help me I'll...

PAT
What, I got a death wish?

LEO
So I take the shower, change my pants, put on that fancy shirt I got with the kangaroo on the pocket...

PAT
You changed your pants?

LEO
Wouldn't you?

PAT
Never after noontime.

LEO
I get to the room, I look at her card to make sure I got the right one. I turn the card over and guess what it says.

PAT
"Smile, you're on Candid Camera."

LEO
It says "Genevieve Goodwin...

PAT
Yeah?

LEO
"Pastor...

PAT
Yeah...what?

LEO
"First Congregationalist Church, Windsor Locks, Connecticut."

PAT
What?

LEO
She's a minister!

PAT
This is too much!

LEO
Pickin' up guys in the casino.

PAT
Goddamn Protestants.

LEO
I'm tellin' ya, I'm headin' back to that elevator in seconds flat.

PAT
I would hope so.

LEO
A few years ago, the legs in better shape, I woulda made it.

PAT
Whatdya mean, she...she...

LEO
She opens her door, sees me pressin' the button. She's standin' there in her pajama.

PAT
Her pajamas?

LEO
Pajama. Just the top.

PAT
Blow my nose and pass the Kaopectate.

LEO
Pat, I'm tellin' ya, that medicine I was talkin' about...?

PAT
The Viagra?

LEO
Didn't need it. One look at that doorway--pop goes the weasel.

PAT
I'm speechless.

LEO
She's givin' me one of these...
    (indicates Red summoning him to
     her room)
...I look around. Nobody in the corridor. Nobody sees nothin'. I figure--what the hell...

PAT
Leo!

LEO
What have I got to lose!

PAT
You're kidding me!

LEO
I head for the room.

PAT
The balls you got!

LEO
She gets me inside, she shuts the door. She turns off the light. She got a candle goin' on the table next to the bed. She got a bottle of wine and two glasses on the table. She sashays around the bed. When she moves, her perfume kinda...takes over the room. Smells like she fell into a vat of melted Chicklets. She lifts up the glasses, walks over to me, gives me a glass. I feel like a real shit but I can't help myself. Then the guilt takes over. "I'm married," I tell her. "My wife ain't dead." "I know," she says. "I always know when they're lying," she says. "I don't care," she says. She takes a sip outa the glass. She walks over to the radio, turns it on. One of them oldies stations. She puts the glass down. She flops down on the bed.

He stops. He and Pat are now staring in their minds at the sight on the bed. Pat waits. Nothing.

PAT
Well...go ahead! What did you do!!!

LEO
Nothin'.

PAT
Nothin'?

LEO
Nothin'. I'm standin' there. She's stretched out on the bed. Reverend Genevieve. Lookin' like Sharon Gless before she let herself go.

PAT
Was she Cagney or Lacey?

                    LEO
Who gives a shit! I mean, she is...spectacular. I take a step towards
her. I'm not even thinkin' anymore. And then...

                    PAT
And then?

                    LEO
And then...the radio.

                    PAT
What about the radio?

                    LEO
The song. They played the song.

                    PAT
Oh, shit.

                    LEO
"Only You."

                    PAT
Get outa here. Get...OUTA here!

                    LEO
Like a sign.

                    PAT
Unbefreakin'lievable.

                    LEO
I just walk outa the room. Down the stairs. Don't even wait for the
elevator. Back to the casino. Over to the slots. She's there, yankin' at
that thing like there's no tomorrow. I walk up behind her. Tap her
on the back. She turns. Looks at me.

                    PAT
What does she say?

                    LEO
She says, "What's with the changin' your pants?"

                    PAT
               (beat, smiles)
Gert.

                    LEO
Yeah. Yeah.

                    PAT
          (beat)
Your song.

                    LEO
"Only You."

                    PAT
Son of a bitch.

                    A long moment. Each man stares straight
                    ahead.

                    LEO
And they say God is dead.

                    PAT
Who says that?

                    LEO
I dunno. Just an expression. Don't mean anything.

                    PAT
          (beat)
You think you can walk straight now?

                    LEO
I think.

                    PAT
Let's go.

                    They rise, move away a bit, past the front
                    porch.

                    PAT (cont'd)
You're gonna get hell.

                    LEO
I know.

                    PAT
Me too.

                    LEO
I know.

                    PAT
I guess it's good.

                    LEO
What?

                    PAT
That there's hell to get. From somebody.

                    LEO
                (beat)
I guess.

                    PAT
                (stops, looks to sky)
So...is there?

                    LEO
Is there what?

                    PAT
A God? Up there? Watchin' us? Takin' care of us? Is there? You think?

                    LEO
                (beat)
Let me put it this way, Pat...

                        Unseen to them, Alma's front door opens.
                        Alma stands behind the screen door and
                        watches them.

                    LEO (cont'd)
                (puts his arm around Pat's
                    shoulder)
If I ever wonder about that...if it ever crosses my mind to think, even for a split second, that God don't exist, I'm just gonna stop myself...

                    PAT
You're gonna stop yourself.

LEO
And I'm gonna sing...
    (starts to sing)
"Only you...can-a make this world seem right...Only you..."

Pat joins him in song. They walk around the corner, into the night, singing. They are not walking very straight.

As they disappear, Alma opens the screen door, and steps onto the porch. We see now that she is carrying an old hat box, which clearly has something in it. She steps to her chair on the porch, and sits. Perhaps we can still hear the boys, slightly, in the distance. She sits a moment, holding the box, taking in the neighborhood. It becomes very silent. She opens the box, looks into it, reaches in and touches something in the box, then closes it again. She takes the box to her breast, and cradles it. She starts to rock slowly in the chair, back and forth, back and forth...

<u>*And the LIGHTS fade to black.*</u>

Scene Five

The following morning, ten o'clock or so. Marjorie and Pat approach from around the corner. Marjorie carries a large envelope, and is leading the way, which is, of course, the way God intended it to be.

PAT
I still don't get it. You're gonna see her this afternoon!

MARJORIE
I want to do this now.

PAT
    (looks at house)
She's not home.

MARJORIE

She's home.

PAT

I'm tellin' ya, that's an empty house.

MARJORIE

You can tell that's an empty house.

PAT

I can.

MARJORIE

Just by looking at it.

PAT

I can.

MARJORIE

How?

PAT

It's a gift. She's not home.

MARJORIE
(goes to door)
She's home. She told me she'd be home this mornin'. It's this mornin'. Alma said she'd be home, she's home.
(finds a note taped to the door)

PAT

What does it say?

MARJORIE

She's not home.

PAT

Let's go.

MARJORIE
(read)
"Had to run to CVS. Back in ten minutes."
(considers, then sits)

PAT
(beat)
What, we're waitin'?

MARJORIE
Ten minutes.

PAT
(beat)
Me too?

MARJORIE
It won't kill you. I'm not keepin' this raffle money in the house. I want to give it to her. She's the treasurer.
(beat, Pat pouts)
After last night, you're gonna give me grief? Nine minutes now. Sit.

Reluctantly, he trudges very slowly to the chair on the porch and sits. There is no talking. There is only staring ahead. The impression we should get is that they have pretty much run out of things to talk about, although this doesn't seem to bother them. Nothing is said for a significant amount of time.

MARJORIE (cont'd)
You know what would be a good idea?

PAT
What?

MARJORIE
If we renewed our marriage vows.

PAT
(beat; slow head turn to her)
What, like in front of people?

MARJORIE
Friends and family, yes.

PAT
(longer beat)
See, this is why we should never talk without other people around.

MARJORIE
What's wrong with renewing our marriage vows? It's romantic.

PAT
It's unnecessary. That's why they call them vows. So you don't have to do them more than once. Gives you time to do other things.

MARJORIE
What other things?

PAT
(beat)
I don't know. Bowl?
(beat)
Exercise?

MARJORIE
(skeptically)
What would you do to exercise?

PAT
(beat, considers)
Bowl?
(beat)
How much time left?

Another long moment of staring and not talking. Eventually, Marjorie starts the ball rolling again.

MARJORIE
Would you marry me now?

PAT
What?

MARJORIE
If we weren't already married, would you marry me now?

PAT
(beat)
You mean now the way you look now?

MARJORIE
Yes.

PAT
(beat)
What do I look like?

MARJORIE
What?

PAT
If I'm decidin' whether to marry you now the way you look, what do I look like?

MARJORIE
You look like you.

PAT
(long beat)
All right, then, yes. I would marry you.

Marjorie beams a smile and looks straight ahead. Pat smiles, then turns away, rolling his eyes. Marjorie doesn't see this.

MARJORIE
(beat)
Well, what if you didn't look like you look?

PAT
What would I look like?

MARJORIE
Paul Newman.

PAT
(likes this at first, then thinks about it)
Paul Newman now?

MARJORIE

Yes. Now.

PAT

He's eighty.

MARJORIE

Yes.

PAT

You think he's better looking than I am?

MARJORIE
(long beat, then carefully)

Yes.

PAT

Even now?

MARJORIE
(another long beat, then a little less
   carefully)

Yes.

PAT

Okay, then, you say that, he's so adorable, then, yes, if I look like him I don't marry you.

MARJORIE

Oh.

PAT

So.

MARJORIE

So...who do you marry?

PAT

If I look like Paul Newman?

MARJORIE

Yes.

PAT
(thinks hard, then smiles)

Lara Flynn Boyle.

MARJORIE
Who?

PAT
The prosecutor. On The Practice. Is that still on?

MARJORIE
That skinny thing?

PAT
Hey, if Leo can sleep with her, I can marry her.

MARJORIE
What?

PAT
Never mind.
              (beat)
We should stop talking.

MARJORIE
Fine.

Another long silence with staring. Again, Marjorie breaks it.

MARJORIE (cont'd)
          (finally)
Tony Danza.

PAT
What?

MARJORIE
You pick Lara Flynn Boyle. I pick Tony Danza.

PAT
Pick for what?

MARJORIE
For marrying if I look like...not me now.

PAT
(beat; thinks)
So if I'm Paul Newman for Lara Flynn Boyle, who are you for Tony Danza?

MARJORIE
(thinks)
Raquel Welch.

PAT
Raquel Welch.

MARJORIE
Raquel Welch.

PAT
Hmm.
(really thinks this one through,
stares at Marjorie)
We should go home right now.

MARJORIE
Why? Alma will be...
(he stares at her; she catches on a
little)
Oh!
(she catches on a lot)
Oh!!!!

PAT
Put the raffle money in the mail slot and let's get outa here.
(steps off the porch)

MARJORIE
(rising)
You think?

PAT
I think.

MARJORIE
You mean it?

PAT
I mean it. The Globe is on the doorstep.

                    MARJORIE
What?

                    PAT
Put the money in the slot. Come on...

                    MARJORIE
          (places money in slot, closes door,
            looks to Pat)
This is like Christmas!

                    PAT
Deck the halls, baby.

                         *Marjorie giggles and joins Pat at the bottom of
                         the stairs. They both giggle like children and
                         start to skip away. Suddenly, Marjorie stops.*

                    MARJORIE
Wait!

                    PAT
What?

                    MARJORIE
Wait...just a minute...

                    PAT
I hate to break this to you, but time is not on our side...

                    MARJORIE
If we go home...

                    PAT
Yeah?

                    MARJORIE
And do...this...thing...

                    PAT
Yeah? Yeah? If we go home and do this thing, what?

                    MARJORIE
          (beat)
Am I...gonna be me?

PAT

What?

MARJORIE

Or am I gonna be...Raquel Welch?

PAT
(absorbs this; then, with meaning)

Who do you wanna be?

MARJORIE
(absorbs this; then begins to get it;
she smiles)

Okay.
(beat)
And who are you?

PAT
(a reasonable Danza imitation)

Hey! You're da boss!

MARJORIE
(giggly again)

Let's go!
(they start off)

> *Alma arrives, bearing three CVS bags, and approaches the porch.*

MARJORIE (cont'd)
(runs, then stops)

The raffle money is in the slot! We'll be back for the cookout!

PAT

Hurry up, Raquel!

MARJORIE

Coming Tony!!!

ALMA
(as they disappear; beat; then, with
a shrug)

Somebody's gonna get hurt...

*She continues to walk towards the porch.
Inside the house, the TELEPHONE RINGS. As
soon as she hears it, Alma picks up her pace.*

                    ALMA (cont'd)
              (to herself)
Oh, Jeez...

*She gets to the door, drops the CVS bags,
struggles to find her keys...*

                    ALMA (cont'd)
Don't hang up.
              (refers to keys, phone keeps ringing)
Where are you?
              (yells)
Don't hang up! Ah!
              (finds keys, struggles to open the
              door)
I gotta get a machine...
              (yells)
Don't hang up!

*She opens the door and reaches inside to get
the cordless phone, which is right near the
door. She steps back on the porch to grab one
of her dropped CVS bags as she answers the
phone.*

                    ALMA (cont'd)
Hello?...Yes...Yes...Thank you for calling me back...I didn't think you
would till tomorrow...Labor Day and all...Look...I wanted to ask you
about your article this morning...

*She moves to the table on the porch, where she
will find a newspaper.*

                    ALMA (cont'd)
              (reads; article is on the front page;
              this is not easy)
I was wonderin' if...you could tell me where I could find him...
              (beat)
I don't want to say. I just want to know where he is.
              (refers to paper)

                    ALMA (cont'd)
Why not?...What do you mean HIS privacy?...
          (becoming angry)
I know you're a journalist, you write for the paper, you're a
journalist. I know. I'm not stupid. Just tell me where he is...
          (beat)
It's none of your business why.
          (beat)
Yeah? Well...I'm just doin' *my* job.
          (beat)
Never mind. Never mind. I shoulda known. Just...just...
          (beat; takes a breath)
...If you talk to him again...if you see him...just...tell him...tell him I
know...Never mind who, just tell him you talked to a lady and the
lady said, "I know what you did."...No. No, don't call me back. No.

>   *Abruptly, she hangs up. She takes a deep*
>   *breath, gathers her bags, and goes inside.*
>
>   *Blackout*
>
>   *End of Act One*
>
>   *Act Two*
>
>   *Scene One*
>
>   *Faint sounds of family cookout revelry from*
>   *the back yard. Gert appears from around the*
>   *side of the house. She wields a paper plate*
>   *with picnic food on it, and a soft drink in a*
>   *paper cup. She peeks around the side of the*
>   *house, sees that the porch is empty. She*
>   *breathes a sigh of relief.*

                    GERT
          (to herself)
Thank God.
          (yells around back)
Marjorie! Marjorie! It's empty! I'm gonna sit!...
          (waits for response; we hear
            Marjorie's voice, unintelligible, in
            the distance)
Yeah...well...Whatever...

                              GERT (cont'd)
                         (mumbles as she continues to porch)
I'm sure whatever you said it was pithy.

>   *Gert makes her way to her lawn chair on the
>   porch. She spills two or three ounces of her
>   drink along the way.*

                              GERT (cont'd)
Shit.

>   *She steps off again, spills again, this time on
>   the porch.*

                              GERT (cont'd)
Shit.

>   *She finishes her journey to the chair, puts
>   what's left of the drink on the side table,
>   plunks herself solidly into her chair, and looks
>   at her plate of food.*

                              GERT (cont'd)
                         (whining)
Oh, shit again! Shit! Shit! Shit! Shit!....

>   *Alma appears in the screen door. She wears an
>   apron. She seems to be a bit out of sorts.*

                              ALMA
                         (steps onto the porch)
Hey...hey! Kids in the back yard.
                         (whispers)
What are you shittin' about?

                              GERT
I got a plate. I forgot the potato salad.

                              ALMA
I'll get you some. Whose you want? We got Gerard's and we got Dorothy's from Bingo.

                        GERT
Gimme Gerard's. Dorothy cooks like she plays Bingo. Under the B...
              (Bronx cheer; Alma takes plate)

                        ALMA
I'll be back.

                        GERT
You work too hard.

                      MARJORIE
              (off, from around the side of the
                  house)
Gert!

                        ALMA
They don't call it Labor Day for nothin'.
              (she enters the house)

                        GERT
              (yells to side of house)
On the porch!

                      MARJORIE
              (appears from side of house)
It's like a carnival back there!
              (heads to her chair on the porch)

                        GERT
Alma has enough grandchildren to fill the bleachers at Fenway Park.
She may not know about sex, but her kids picked it up someplace.

                      MARJORIE
Grandchildren happen when you have six kids.

                        GERT
Seven.

                      MARJORIE
Well...seven...sorry. I just...well...right...seven.

                            We hear rustling behind the screen door. Gert
                            ssh's Marjorie, for some reason.

               ALMA
          (appears at door, with plate)
Here you go.
               (gives plate to Gert)
               GERT
Thank you, dear.

               MARJORIE
Alma, sit! You haven't stopped running around for three hours.

               ALMA
I'll sit when everybody leaves.
               (she leaves through door)

               GERT
               (a little snidely)
Gerard certainly knows his way around the kitchen.

               MARJORIE
Oh, stop it.

               GERT
Gerard would have made somebody a lovely wife.

               MARJORIE
Stop. He's not like that.

               GERT
He's not?

               MARJORIE
He's not.

               GERT
How do you know?

               MARJORIE
I asked him.

               GERT
You asked him? When?

               MARJORIE
Just last week. At the cake sale down't the hall.

GERT
What did you say?

MARJORIE
I said, "Gerard, do you like men?"

GERT
I can't believe you asked him that. What did he say?

MARJORIE
I remember exactly what he said. He said "I like men. I like women. I like dogs. I like cats. I like porcelain figurines, I like Moo Goo Gai pan and I like a cold shower on a hot night."

GERT
This is an answer?

MARJORIE
It was for me.

GERT
What did it mean?

MARJORIE
(very directly, to Gert)
In a sweet way, it meant mind your own business.

GERT
Oh.

MARJORIE
So.

GERT
So...I'd be wastin' my time tryin' to set him up.

MARJORIE
Who with?

GERT
Alma.

MARJORIE
Why would you want to set Alma up with Gerard if you thought he was homosexual?

GERT
I thought she might be able to shift him into reverse.
(shift gesture)

MARJORIE
Oh, please...

GERT
Alma is a very attractive woman.

MARJORIE
You're looney.

GERT
Can you imagine the parties those two would give?

Leo slams onto the porch from the door.

LEO
I'm leavin'.

GERT
You're not leavin'.

LEO
Since when you make my decisions for me?

GERT
Since July 23rd, 1962.

MARJORIE
It was a lovely wedding.

LEO
Too many kids out there. Mean kids, too. Nasty kids.

GERT
Get a plate.

LEO
One of 'em called me an old poop.

GERT
You are an old poop. Get a plate.

LEO
I already had a plate. I wanna go home and take a pill.

GERT
You'll go home when I go home and we'll both take a pill.
        (to Marjorie)
I think we should do it anyway.

MARJORIE
Do what?

LEO
Do what?

GERT
Set 'em up.

MARJORIE
Who?

LEO
Who?

GERT
Him and Alma.

MARJORIE
Oh, no! Gerard?

LEO
Set 'em up? You mean like together?

GERT
I think we should.

LEO
What're you nuts?
        (to Marjorie)
Don't she know?

MARJORIE
She knows.

                    LEO
                (to Gert)
What're you bored? You don't get enough entertainment for
yourself? Rent a video, for crissakes.

                    GERT
I'm only lookin' at two lonely people and I'm tryin' to make 'em less
lonely is all I'm doin'.

                    MARJORIE
Who says they're lonely?

                    GERT
They're lonely.

                    MARJORIE
But it's like...there's a...a basic...incompatibility there that...

                    LEO
Yeah! The incompatible thing, there. What're you gonna do about
that?

                    GERT
They're incompatible in only one aspect of a potential relationship.

                    MARJORIE
A pretty big aspect.

                    GERT
What big? What's to do in that department at their age, huh?

                    LEO
Ain't that the truth.

                    GERT
                (shoots Leo a look, chooses to ignore
                    him)
What're they missin' there? Big deal! The important thing is
companionship, ain't it?

                    MARJORIE
Well...

GERT

Well...And wouldn't they hit it off? Wouldn't they? They're both neat.

MARJORIE

And clean.

GERT

They both love the parties and the gettin' together and the cookin' and the washin' and the fixin' up.

MARJORIE

I suppose.

GERT

Leo.

LEO

What?

GERT

Get him out here.

LEO

Me?

GERT

Yes, you.

LEO

You're gonna do this now?

GERT

I could be dead tomorrow.

LEO

Promises. Promises.

GERT

Go.

LEO
(rising, to door)
You're wastin' your time.
(stops)
They tried this with Liberace, you know.

GERT
Get!
(he leaves)

MARJORIE
What in God's name are you going to do to Gerard?

GERT
Don't know yet. I'm wingin' it.

MARJORIE
He's very sensitive.

GERT
I can be sensitive.

MARJORIE
Yeah? When were you ever sensitive?

GERT
You'd be surprised.

MARJORIE
You bet I'd be surprised.

GERT
Oh, you're pushin' me now.

MARJORIE
Sensitive? You?

GERT
You gonna keep pushin'?

MARJORIE
Dream on. Sensitive.
(a dismissive sound)
Psh.

GERT
Okay. All right. I'm pushed.
(leans in)
Let me tell you about the time Leo changed his pants.

MARJORIE
Excuse me?

GERT
You remember Foxwoods, in February?

MARJORIE
Sure. The bus. We saw Steve and Edyie.

GERT
You did. I didn't.

MARJORIE
They're very talented.

GERT
(shrugging it off)
Eh...whatever...Anyway, when you're at the show, I'm at the slots.

MARJORIE
You and your slots.

GERT
I'm keepin' an eye on Leo. He's at the Blackjack. He thinks I don't know what he's doin'. I let him think.

MARJORIE
Sure.

GERT
About 10, 10:30 I see him gettin' into the elevator.

MARJORIE
Yeah? So?

GERT
With Genevieve Goodwin.

MARJORIE
(shocked)
No!

GERT
The Pick-em-up Pastor.

MARJORIE
She was there?

GERT
Of course she was there. You think she'd miss Valentine's Week at Foxwoods?

MARJORIE
I suppose not.

GERT
Never! So I see him get into the elevator.

MARJORIE
Did you follow him?

GERT
(an explanation not to be
challenged)
I was on the slots!

MARJORIE
Oh. Sure.

GERT
I sent Rose to follow him.

MARJORIE
Rose followed him?

GERT
She has no money, so she never has anything to do at Foxwoods.

MARJORIE
So what happened?

GERT
Ten minutes later, Rose is back in the casino. She tells me Leo went to our room, but then he came out again. Wearin' different pants.

MARJORIE
Different pants...

GERT
Rose is very observant. She hid in a corner of the hallway and when he got on the elevator she heard him tell whoever was on the buttons that he was going to the sixth floor. I check with the desk. Genevieve is on the sixth floor.

MARJORIE
My goodness.

GERT
Time to leave the slots.

MARJORIE
I would think.

GERT
I get her room number. I go to the sixth floor. Hallway is empty. I stand outside her room. All I can hear is the radio.

MARJORIE
How do you know Leo's in there?

GERT
He's got a smell.

MARJORIE
Ah.

GERT
Cigars, Life Savers and Budweiser. He might as well wear a cow bell.

MARJORIE
Okay.

GERT
So I wait. And I wait. All I'm hearin' is the radio. I'm thinkin' about bustin' in the door, but the sciatica was brutal that night, so I figured I'd give it a few more minutes.

MARJORIE
You're very brave.

GERT
So it's quiet. Too quiet. But it's the quiet that's keepin' me hopeful.

MARJORIE
Why?

GERT
Because Leo hasn't had sex without fartin' since 1980.

MARJORIE

So the quiet is good.

GERT

From my standpoint. So I wait. And I listen. And then...

MARJORIE

Then?

GERT

Then...it happened.

MARJORIE

What happened?

GERT

I heard the song. On the radio.

MARJORIE

What song?

GERT

You ready?

MARJORIE

Gert!

GERT

"Only You."

MARJORIE

No!

GERT

Yes! As soon as I hear it, I tear ass down the hallway and hide behind one of them fake ferns. Just as I duck down, I hear Genevieve's door open.

MARJORIE

Is it Leo?

GERT

It's Leo. I peek out from behind a fern leaf. He's backin' out of the room. Coughin' and stammerin'. "I'm sorry," he's sayin'. "I can't.

GERT (cont'd)
I just can't do this." And he skitters over to the elevator. He presses the button, but it doesn't come fast enough--which was never one of his problems, by the way...

MARJORIE
Oh, you!

GERT
So I see him goin' for the stairs. I run over and catch his elevator and get back to my seat at the slots, 'cause I know that's where he's goin'.

MARJORIE
And is it?

GERT
Oh, yeah. He's outa breath and ready to pass out but he comes right over to me at the slots and stands there like he was my pet puppy and he missed me.

MARJORIE
So..what'd you do?

GERT
Nothin'. That's what I done. Nothin'. Just went on with life and made out like nothin' ever happened. Because nothin' did.
(beat; leans in)
Sensitive. Don't you think that makes me sensitive?

MARJORIE
It makes you...something. I'm not sure what I call it.

GERT
Well, I call it sensitive. And besides, now...if I ever need it...for any reason at all...there it is!

Leo and Pat enter from around the back of the house.

LEO
He ain't comin'.

GERT
Whatdya mean he ain't comin'? Did you say somethin' to him?

                    LEO

No.

                    GERT
          (to Pat)
Did he?

                    PAT

Yes.

                    LEO
          (whacking Pat on the arm)
I told him what you were up to and he said thanks he can make his own potato salad.

                　　MARJORIE

Thank God.

                    GERT

His loss.

                    LEO
          (to Pat)
Okay. Tell her what you told me.

                    PAT

Now?

                    LEO

Now.
          (to Gert)
Pat has somethin' to tell you.

                    GERT

Yeah? What?

                    PAT

Uh...I'm heading home and...uh...I need Leo to come with me to help me to...uh...

                    LEO

Pat needs me to fix the dribble in his toilet.

MARJORIE
There's a dribble in the toilet?

GERT
There's no dribble in anybody's toilet.

PAT
Oh, there's a distinct dribble.
(to Marjorie)
Started after you left the house to come over here to help Alma set up. Big dribble. Major dribble.

MARJORIE
Well, can't you just jiggle it if it's a dribble? Isn't that what you do when something doesn't work--jiggle it.

PAT
(considers this)
Oh, this dribble is way beyond jigglin'.

GERT
(to Leo)
What do you know about dribbles?

LEO
You know damn well, when there's a dribble at our house, I'm the one who fixes it.

GERT
I never heard a dribble at our house.

LEO
I work very fast.

GERT
There's no dribble. There's a game. On the TV.

LEO
There's a dribble.

GERT
Game!

LEO
Dribble!

GERT

Game!

LEO

Dribble!

GERT

Oh, get outa here, the both of ya.

LEO
(smiles, moves)

Let's go, Pat!
(they start off)

GERT

Just don't go away thinkin' you're puttin' anything over on me.

LEO

Oh, I'd never try to put anything over on you, sweetheart.
(with a sly smile to Pat, who gently
acknowledges it)

GERT

Leo!
(Leo and Pat stop)
I have one more thing to say before you go.

LEO

What's that, angel face?

GERT
(sings)
"Only you can-a make this world seem right..."

Leo looks askance at Pat. Pat catches on.

PAT
(to Leo)
See what happens when you change your pants?

Pat shoves the stunned Leo and they skitter away.

MARJORIE
(to Gert)
You're very good.

GERT

I'm a pro.

Alma enters through the screen door.

ALMA

Well, that's the funniest thing...

MARJORIE

What, Alma?

ALMA

I just went up to Gerard to thank him for all his help and he ran away so fast I thought it was a Maalox Moment or somethin'. Got in his car, drove off goin' like sixty.

MARJORIE

Gert's fault.

GERT

Ssh!

ALMA

What?

MARJORIE

Gert's fault. Blame Gert.

ALMA
(to Gert)

What'd you do?

GERT

Oh, I told Leo I wanted to talk to Gerard about something and Leo told Gerard before I could tell Gerard and it scared Gerard away.

ALMA

Tell Gerard what?

GERT

That he's lonesome and you're lonesome and you should both stop being lonesome and you should do it together.

ALMA
What? You were settin' us up?

GERT
Somethin' like that.

MARJORIE
Exactly like that.

ALMA
(sits, gently)
Gert...you heard about the center downtown?

GERT
Oh, I know what he is! So what? You both need a companion. I thought it was a good idea.

ALMA
Oh. Well, sure. I suppose that's a good idea. If you need one.

GERT
You don't need one?

ALMA
I have one.

GERT
Who? Us? We don' count. We smell different from the kind of companion you need.

ALMA
Look...listen to me...Tom. Tom will always be my companion. I know, he's not sittin' across from me at the table with the paper in his face or screamin' at me to shut my trap when I'm tellin' him to take a right turn. I know he's not gonna be doin' my shoppin' anymore, or pickin' up the wrong kind of detergent at the Market Basket. But he's around. All over the place. All the time. And nobody can tell me he's not around.
(to Gert)
Not even you could tell me that.

MARJORIE
That's nice, Alma. That's really, really nice.

                    GERT
I was only tryin' to help.

                    ALMA
          (a bit brusquely, gathers Gert's
            plate, etc.)
I know you were. But do me a favor. Don't help me anymore like that.

              She goes inside.

                    GERT
What got her bloomers in a bunch?

                    MARJORIE
          (knowingly)
Well...

                    GERT
Well what?
          (thinks, gets it)
Oh. You think?

                    MARJORIE
Well, it's either that or Tom.

                    GERT
I suppose.

                    MARJORIE
Or both.

                    GERT
We should stay, then?

                    MARJORIE
I think.

                    GERT
Till it's over.

                    MARJORIE
Oh, yeah.

                    GERT
Yeah...

They sit, staring straight ahead, as...

<u>*LIGHTS fade to black.*</u>

Scene Two

A little later. Gert and Marjorie are still in their chairs, reading newspapers. Neither is flipping pages. Each seems to be focused on a particular page. After a moment, Gert breaks the silence.

GERT (cont'd)
(still focused on newspaper)
So...whatdya think?

MARJORIE
(also continues to focus on paper)
What do I think about what?

GERT

You're readin' the same paper I'm readin'. I'm askin' you what do you think?
(no response; she continues to read
paper as she speaks)
You have an opinion. I know you have an opinion. There ain't a time when you ain't got an opinion and of all times to have an opinion, this is one of them times. So I'm askin' for your opinion. What do you think?

MARJORIE
(puts down paper)
Well, I think...

GERT
(slaps paper down on her lap)
Let me tell you what *I* think.

MARJORIE
(a sigh)
Why do I even bother...?

GERT

I think it's not natural.

MARJORIE
Well, of course it's not natural. My God, Gert, the children...

GERT
I'm not talkin' about the children. I'm talkin' about the priests.

MARJORIE
So am I.

GERT
Well, I'm talkin' about it's not natural what they expect them to do.

MARJORIE
The priests?

GERT
The priests.

MARJORIE
You mean the no sex.

GERT
I mean the no sex. It's not natural.

MARJORIE
Well, it may not be natural, but it's a vow and they didn't have to take the vow if they didn't want to...do the no sex.

GERT
Well, you know what that is, dontcha?

MARJORIE
What?

GERT
That's bullshit.

MARJORIE
(looking off, warningly)
Gert!

GERT
Oh, she's inside.

MARJORIE
You know she's in a bad mood.

GERT
I know. I know. It's his birthday tomorrow.

MARJORIE
Yes.

GERT
Richie.

MARJORIE
So don't upset her anymore than she...

GERT
Oh, I can say bullshit if something's bullshit and this is bullshit.

MARJORIE
It's a sacred vow.

GERT
It's a bullshit vow.

MARJORIE
A vow is a promise.

GERT
It is.

MARJORIE
A holy promise.

GERT
A vow is a promise, yes.

MARJORIE
A vow is a vow.

GERT
I agree.

MARJORIE
Well...

GERT
(beat)
Unless it's a bullshit vow.

MARJORIE

Gert...

GERT

Listen to me...Listen to me now 'cause I'm gonna say somethin's gonna shock you.

MARJORIE

Oh, please, don't...

GERT

I <u>know</u>, I'm tellin' ya. I <u>know</u> that outa them vows they take, outa the Big Three...

MARJORIE

What big three?

GERT

The poverty, chastity and obedience.

MARJORIE

Ah.

GERT

I <u>know</u>--from a personal experience fact--I know that outa them vows, number one and number three are kids' stuff compared to number two.

MARJORIE

Number two.

GERT

Chastity.

MARJORIE

That's the tough one according to you.

GERT

The toughest. From a personal experience fact, I know this.

MARJORIE

You think chastity is too much for them to handle?

GERT
You might as well ask them to pee through their ears.

MARJORIE
(back to paper)
I don't want to know, you know.

GERT
You don't want to know what?

MARJORIE
I don't want to know about your personal experience fact.

GERT
Well, then you can wallow in your ignorance because I got meat and potatoes to back up my fact.
(back to paper, beat)
I'm just tellin' you that when push comes to shove and they gotta choose between listenin' to the Pope or listenin' to that little fella in the middle of their pants...

MARJORIE
Good Lord, Gert...

GERT
It's the little fella gets the nod every time.

MARJORIE
(Gert is really getting to her)
That's just...That's just...

GERT
Come on, Marjorie, spill it. I don't start these things just to hear myself talk.

MARJORIE
(drops paper)
I think that's just...just...

GERT
Bullshit. You think it's bullshit. Say it. It'll be good for ya. Bullshit. Say it. Say bullshit.

MARJORIE
Well that's what it is!

GERT

What's what it is?

MARJORIE
(beat, then, with great difficulty)

Bullshit!

GERT

Good for you! Now...back it up!

MARJORIE

What?

GERT

Back it up! You think what I'm sayin' is bullshit, prove it to me. When I say somethin's bullshit I back it up with personal experience facts, even though you don't want to hear 'em. You say what I'm sayin' is bullshit, give me some reasons.

MARJORIE

The priests I know do not...have not...succumbed to the temptations of the flesh.

GERT

Oh, they haven't.

MARJORIE

No.

GERT

None of the priests you know. Not one of them has jumped the fence on a lonely Saturday night.

MARJORIE
(beat)

That I know of. No.

Gert raises paper to read. As does Marjorie. Gert whistles the first line of "Beautiful Dreamer." Marjorie drops paper to her lap.

MARJORIE (cont'd)

What!

                        GERT
I thought you didn't want to hear.

                        MARJORIE
                    (paper up)
I don't.

                        Gert whistles the second line of "Beautiful
                        Dreamer." Then stops. Marjorie waits a
                        second, drops her newspaper to make sure Gert
                        has stopped. Satisfied, she lifts the newspaper
                        to her face again. As she does, Gert's whistle
                        explodes back into the song.

                        MARJORIE (cont'd)
                    (drops newspaper)
WHAT!

                        GERT
                    (drops paper)
Personal experience fact.

                        MARJORIE
All right! All right! Tell me! Jesus, Mary and Joseph.

                        GERT
Okay. Good.
                    (beat)
I'm gonna throw a name at you now and I don't want you to bite my head off when I throw it.

                        MARJORIE
Just...throw it.

                        GERT
Father...

                        MARJORIE
Yes? Father. Father who?

                        GERT
                    (long beat)
McAndrews.

MARJORIE
(slaps paper back up)

Oh! No!

GERT

No?

MARJORIE

No. No! I won't believe it! No! Not him! No! I won't listen! No! No! No!

Marjorie keeps the paper in front of her face. Gert stares right through the paper at her. A long moment of Gert burning her eyes through the paper until Marjorie can't take it anymore and slaps her paper down.

MARJORIE (cont'd)

Oh! What!

GERT

You remember him with the guitar.

MARJORIE

Sure. The guitar. He started with all the folk masses back then. He was always with the guitar. The Cumbayah.

GERT

The Cumbayah. Exactly.

MARJORIE

I don't think a Sunday went by the four years he was here he didn't do the Cumbayah at all the masses.

GERT

He was fond of the song, no doubt about that.

MARJORIE

Cumbayah.
(wistfully)
Sunday after Sunday.

GERT
(also wistfully)
Sunday after Sunday. Cumbayah.

MARJORIE
(beat)
God, I hated that song.

GERT
Anyway, you remember the Sunday his string broke?

MARJORIE
Who?

GERT
McAndrews.

MARJORIE
His string broke?

GERT
The string on his guitar.

MARJORIE
Oh. Yes! And it nearly took out the eye of that altar boy.

GERT
Timmy Provencher. Little French boy. Little brat.

MARJORIE
The ambulance drove up on the church lawn, I remember.

GERT
It did. And then McAndrews got in the ambulance with the little snot. Remember?

MARJORIE
What about it?

GERT
Well, do you remember how much longer he lasted in the parish after his string broke?

MARJORIE
I don't know. Couple of months only.

GERT
Five weeks. And he was supposed to stay two more years.

MARJORIE

What's your point?

GERT

My point is that McAndrews stayed in the hospital all night to make sure Timmy Provencher's eye was all right. And the word came down to me personally that at about three a.m. in the morning McAndrews was playin' Cumbayah again.

MARJORIE

In the hospital?

GERT

In a utility closet with a night nurse named Brenda who didn't seem to mind that he was pluckin' his Cumbayah on only five strings.

MARJORIE

What are you drivin' at?

GERT

I'm drivin' at a week later he volunteered to be Night Chaplain at the hospital.

MARJORIE

Big deal.

GERT

He set up an office in the utility closet.

MARJORIE

You and your...

GERT

And he got his string fixed. Nightly. If you catch my drift.

MARJORIE
(paper up)

I'm not listenin'...

GERT

Two weeks after that, Brenda quits and moves to Port Huron, Michigan.

MARJORIE
(paper down)
What?

GERT
(taps her belly)
Along with her own little night deposit. Next thing you know, McAndrews and his guitar were shipped off to Brazil.

MARJORIE
(with disdain)
Oh...

GERT
Cumbayah in Portuguese.

MARJORIE
And this is your personal experience fact?

GERT
Yes. I answered the phone in the rectory for Rose the week he left. There was much information that week.

MARJORIE
So?

GERT
So, if there's one thing I do, it's retain. I retained.

MARJORIE
I'm sure you did.

GERT
And all this that's happenin' is what happens when you go against the natural.

MARJORIE
Oh, you're way off.

GERT
Am I now?

MARJORIE
What's goin' on with the priests in the paper goes on with everybody else, too. It's not just the priests.

GERT

Is that so?

MARJORIE

It's in every walk of life.

GERT

Is it?

MARJORIE

It is.

GERT

What is?

MARJORIE
(shakes paper)

This! The...
(whispers)
...pedophilia!

GERT

Every walk of life.

MARJORIE

It says here...in the sidebar...see?
(reads)
"A spokesperson for the archdiocese apologized to the victims but cautioned that pedophilia is not limited to the priesthood and that diligent watch must be kept to police other professions as well."

GERT

Right.

MARJORIE

Right.

GERT

Right.
(beat)
Gotta make sure we keep our eyes open for all them pedophilin' plumbers out there.

MARJORIE

Stop it!

GERT

Open your eyes, Marjorie! They're lockin' these poor fellas up in a little room in the rectory with nothin' but their imaginations and Cinemax to keep them busy!

MARJORIE

You're nutty!

GERT

It's time!

MARJORIE

Time for what?

GERT

It's time for them to get somethin' they shoulda been given a long time ago! Time for the church to round up all the priests and single mothers on a Saturday night and do it. Just do it! Bite the bullet and have one!

MARJORIE

Have what?

GERT

A mixer!

MARJORIE

Jesus, Mary and Joseph...

GERT

Well, why not? Couple of times a year. When it's not Christmas or Easter. St. Pat's and Halloween, maybe. Open up the parish hall, hire one of them DJ's and have a mixer for all the priests and the Catholic single mothers. Make some connections. Put an ad in the bulletin. Maybe even the paper. "Single Mothers, Come do the Hustle in a room full of Fathers!" They'll be knocking down the doors.

MARJORIE

Out of your mind.

GERT

There's nothin' sexier than a fella in a Roman collar doin' the Chicken Dance.

MARJORIE
(calling off)
Alma! Are you all right in there?

GERT
And then they let 'em all hook up and get married.

MARJORIE
Alma!

GERT
Never mind the pre-Cana stuff. The marriage lessons. The single mothers already know the drill. What the priests don't know, they can pick up at home in a week.

MARJORIE
Alma!

GERT
Open up all them empty rooms on the third floor of all them rectories. Knock down some walls. Throw together a few kitchenettes.

MARJORIE
Kitchenettes?

GERT
In two or three years you'll have an archdiocese full of instant Catholic families and a lot of happy priests with healthy prostates.

MARJORIE
ALMA!

Alma sticks her head onstage, from inside her house.

ALMA
The yellin'!

MARJORIE
What are you doing?

ALMA
You know what I'm doin'...the macaroons.

GERT

Oh, the macaroons.

MARJORIE

You're cooking again? Everybody's gone...

ALMA

The macaroons are for us, nobody else. I got 'em out of the oven. I'm puttin' 'em on a plate.

MARJORIE

Well...

ALMA

So hold your horses!
    (starts away; stops; with meaning)
Don't rush my macaroons.
    (she is gone)

    Gert still stares in Marjorie's direction, waiting for a reaction. Marjorie works hard to avoid looking at Gert, rustles her newspaper, fidgets. But she can't shake the stare. Finally, Gert speaks.

GERT

You're fightin' it but you know I'm on to something here.

MARJORIE

Look, just...when she comes out here...don't be bringing up that word.

GERT

What word?

MARJORIE

That word! The one we've been talking about!

GERT
    (beat)
Cumbayah?

MARJORIE

Pedophilia!
>(catches herself, whispers)

Pedophilia. The last thing I want to do is try to explain that one to her.

GERT

It'd do her good.

MARJORIE

Oh, you're always looking out for what's good for everybody but yourself.

GERT

Whatdya mean by that?

MARJORIE

I mean it's a private thing is what I mean. I mean it's none of your business with the priests and the nurses and the utility closets.

GERT

Oh, it isn't?

MARJORIE

No, it isn't.

GERT

So tell me this...when the priest is up there on the pulpit and he's tellin' you what you can do and what you can't do and what happens to you if you go ahead and do do what you can't do, what are you supposed to do when you find out he's been doin' what he can't do all the while he's tellin' you you can't do what you want to do?

MARJORIE
>(beat)

What?

GERT

You got the gist.

MARJORIE
>(beat)

Well...it's a faith thing.

GERT
What's a faith thing?

MARJORIE
If we say we're Catholics, then we have to play by the rules. And the rules say we're supposed to have faith in the priests. So you have faith in the priests...and you hope to God...

GERT
Yeah? You hope to God what?

MARJORIE
You hope to God...that the priests you have faith in...don't...
    (shakes the newspaper)
Do this!

GERT
    (long beat)
That's having a lot of faith.

MARJORIE
Well, that's what it takes.

GERT
I don't know.

MARJORIE
What don't you know?

GERT
For myself, now.
    (indicates newspaper)
With all this. I don't know. About the faith.

MARJORIE
Oh, Gert...

GERT
    (holds up newspaper)
Look at 'em. Look at how many.

MARJORIE
I know.

GERT
Yeah, well I <u>don't</u> know.

MARJORIE
All right. Enough. No more talk about this. I don't want to have to explain it all to Alma.

GERT
(skeptically)
Fine. Keep her in the dark.

MARJORIE
Oh, what I wouldn't give to be in the dark myself.

Alma enters. As threatened, she is carrying a tray of macaroons. She offers them to the ladies, each of whom takes one and will munch along as the scene progresses. Alma sets the tray down on a side table without taking a macaroon herself.

MARJORIE (cont'd)
You're not having one?

ALMA
I'm offerin' it up.

GERT
For what?

ALMA
For none of your business.

GERT
You baked a whole tray of macaroons and you're not gonna eat one of 'em?

ALMA
What's the point of offerin' somethin' up if you're gonna make it easy on yourself?

MARJORIE
She's got you there, Gert. These are delicious, Alma.

ALMA
Ain't they always.

MARJORIE
Always. You did a a good job today.

ALMA
Well...

MARJORIE
No, you did. It was hard and you did a good job.

ALMA
It wasn't hard...

MARJORIE
Oh, it was, you had all the grandchildren and...

ALMA
No. That...wasn't hard. Thank you. But no.

MARJORIE
Okay.

ALMA
So. There. What were you talkin' about?

GERT
Just the paper.

ALMA
What's in the paper?

GERT
She wants to know what's in the paper, Marjorie. Tell her what's in the paper.

MARJORIE
(warningly)
Gert...

ALMA
What's in the paper?

MARJORIE
The same old stuff.

GERT
Marjorie wants you to stay inside your shell, Alma.

ALMA
What shell?

GERT
(to Marjorie)

She don't have to be readin' the papers to know what's goin' on, Marjorie. It's all over the TV and the radio and the magazines at the Market Basket. You think you can protect her by keepin' her from readin' the paper, but you can't. If she don't know already, she will soon, no matter how hard you try to keep her uninformed.

MARJORIE
(long beat; considers)

Alma...now...listen to me. I know you've heard things on the radio. Seen 'em on the TV. Bad things. Very bad things. About the priests. Now it is my opinion that you don't need to bother yourself with it. It is far too complicated for any of us to understand. We were brought up in a time when...
(wields paper)
...this...just wasn't talked about. I'm not sayin' it was better we didn't talk about it, I'm just sayin' that we didn't. It's a very, very serious and complex issue, Alma. And I have no intention of trying to explain it to you. So if you ever see the word, or hear the word, don't you even think about it. I don't understand it. Gert doesn't understand it. And you will not understand it.

ALMA
(long beat)

It's Richie's birthday tomorrow, you know.

> *For a moment, all three women say nothing. Clearly, this is a subject that is beyond Gert and Marjorie. Finally, Marjorie speaks. When she does, it is with shock and compassion.*

MARJORIE
Alma...

ALMA
September third. He'd be thirty-four. Imagine that. Richie'd be thirty-four years old tomorrow.

                    GERT
                (carefully)
Do you want to go inside and take a nap, dear?

                    ALMA
No. Why? No, I'm all right. I just...got to thinkin' about Richie and his birthday.

                    MARJORIE
Alma...after all this time...

                    ALMA
He did the thing on his birthday, you know.

                    MARJORIE
Alma...

                    GERT
Go take a nap, sweetheart.

                    MARJORIE
Let her talk, Gert, if she wants to.

                    GERT
I just think...

                    MARJORIE
Let her talk.

                    ALMA
                (long beat)
I got mad at him, you know. We both did. Tom and me both. Mad at him for what he done.
                (beat)
Mainly because we never knew why he done it.
                (beat)
The note he left, it...
                (beat)
Well...we got mad at him.
                (beat)
And then we stopped talkin' about him.

                    MARJORIE
Yes.

ALMA
Well, you know. I never talked about him. Never. About him. Or about what he done.
> (beat)

Did you know I found him?

MARJORIE
No, I didn't. The paper didn't...

ALMA
Oh, the paper. We kept everything out of the paper. "Short illness" we told 'em to put.

GERT
Short illness. I remember.

ALMA
I picked up Susan at her Brownie meeting. Did that every week. We came in the house, Susie and me, and she goes right for the T.V. like she always done, and I seen Richie's baseball glove on the floor of the pantry. He was always leavin' that glove lyin' around. And I was always hollerin' at him to pick it up. So I hollered. "Richie! The glove! How many times do I hafta tell you! Pick up the baseball glove!"
> (beat)

And he didn't answer. Even when I hollered again, he didn't answer. So then I...So I went upstairs and hollered again. Still no answer. His door was closed. I tried to open it. It was locked. His door was locked. Now that got me scared. I'd never known him to lock his door. I didn't even know if there was a key. I knocked a couple of times. Yelled out his name a couple of times. I turned around. Susie's at the top of the stairs, lookin' at me, wonderin' what I'm doin'. I take her hand and we go down the stairs. There's a drawer in the kitchen fulla...everything. Still there now. You know the drawer.

GERT
Sure.

ALMA
I found three or four old keys. Put Susie back in front of the T.V. Brought the keys up the stairs.
> (beat)

The second key opened the door.

                    ALMA (cont'd)
          (long beat)
He used his belt. To do the thing, he used his belt. He was right there when I opened the door. Right there. Hangin' there. One of the old pipes 'cross the top of his room, he used. Kicked the chair away. And done the thing.
          (beat)
My little Richie. My baby boy.
          (long beat)
Short illness. We told the paper.
          (to Gert)
You knew.
          (to Marjorie)
You knew, didn't ya?

                    MARJORIE
There was some talk. We didn't know for sure.

                    ALMA
But you thought...

                    MARJORIE
We thought...yes.

                    ALMA
Well...I'm sorry I didn't...tell it all to you before now.
          (beat)
But now's when I did.
          (long beat, looks toward newspaper
           on table)
"Ask Father Preston." The note he left. That's all it said. "Ask Father Preston."

                    GERT
Father Preston?

          Gert shoots a look to Marjorie, who grabs her own paper to check out the front page.

                    MARJORIE
Oh...dear God...

ALMA
(looks at paper)
A retreat. An altar boys' retreat. In the Berkshires.
(points at paper)
He was there.
(beat)
Richie didn't want to go.
(beat)
I made him go. Told him it would be good for him.
(beat)
A retreat for the altar boys.
(points to paper)
And there he is.
(beat)
I went to him. Back then. Father Preston. The note said "Ask Father Preston," so I did. Drove all the way out to Pittsfield. Found him. And I asked him what Richie mighta meant. No idea, he says. "I have no idea, Mrs. O'Neill" is what he said. And, you know, I remember right then and there, with no good reason, I felt...I said to myself...he's not a priest, this fella. The look in his eyes. Somethin'.
(points to Marjorie's paper)
Priests don't do this. Not the real ones.

Alma looks to her friends. She has forgiven herself. She needs them to help.

ALMA (cont'd)
I...didn't...know...

Her head falls into her lap. Marjorie rises and goes to her, cradling her. Gert joins them. They hold each other, as...

The LIGHTS FADE slowly to black.

Scene Three

Much later that evening. Another quiet, warm late-summer night. Leo and Pat are on the porch, Pat in Marjorie's chair, Leo sitting on the steps. Leo is anxious.

LEO
How long they been in there?

PAT
You remember when you asked me two minutes ago how long?

LEO
You said an hour and a half.

PAT
Add two minutes to that.

They sit a moment, saying nothing. Leo rises.

PAT (cont'd)
Where you goin'?

LEO
School yard. There's a basketball over there. Shoot some hoops.

PAT
You want me go home, get my step ladder?

LEO
It's too bad Ed Sullivan is dead. You could go on right after Topo Gigio.

PAT
Jesus, you're old.

LEO
Ahhh...
   (sits back down: beat)
She been spooky, you know.

PAT
Who?

LEO
Who...Alma.

PAT
Spooky how?

LEO
Spooky like she been one person all her life, then all of a sudden she's another person.

PAT

And you noticed this.

LEO

I'm good at that. Readin' people. What they are. What they're turnin' into.

PAT

Yeah?

LEO

Yeah.

PAT
(beat)
What am I and what am I turnin' into?

LEO
(longer beat)
You're an asshole. And you're turnin' into a bigger asshole.

PAT
(beat; considers)
You are good at that.

LEO

Told ya.

Gert comes out of the house. She seems to have gone through...something.

LEO (cont'd)

So is it over?

GERT
(sits in her chair)
Is what over?

LEO

Whatever it was in there that made you tell us to stay out here.

GERT

Yeah.

LEO

What was it?

                    GERT
Never mind. You're too young.

                    LEO
No, seriously.

                    GERT
Seriously. When you grow up.

                    PAT
Is she okay?

                    GERT
She's okay. She'll be okay.

                    LEO
We don't get no information?

> *Marjorie enters from the house. Also exhausted. She heads for her chair. Pat rises to let her sit.*

                    LEO (cont'd)
              (to Gert, indicating Marjorie and
                  Pat)
<u>She'll</u> tell <u>him</u>.

                    PAT
No, she won't.

                    MARJORIE
No, I won't. And he won't ask.

                    PAT
              (to Leo, as he moves to him)
It's a beautiful thing we got.

                    GERT
What's she up to?

                    MARJORIE
She's on the phone with Susie now. She'll be out in a minute.

                    LEO
Susie? Susie was here all day with the grandkids. She's with her daughter all afternoon, now she's talkin' to her on the phone?

                    MARJORIE
She needed to talk to one of her kids.

                    LEO
Why?
          (Marjorie just waves her hand in
           dismissal; to Pat)
You ask her.

                    PAT
Sure. Watch.
          (to Marjorie)
Why?
          (same hand gesture; then, to Leo)
See?

                    MARJORIE
It's a beautiful thing.

                    LEO
So we don't get to find out nothin'.
          (both Gert and Marjorie do the
           hand wave; to Pat)
What'd I tell ya? They're as spooky as Alma now.

                    MARJORIE
Stop worryin'. She'll be fine.

                    GERT
At least she got the grandkids.

                    MARJORIE
          (affirming)
She's got the grandkids.

                    LEO
She got nothin' but grandkids.

                    GERT
Ssh.

                    LEO
The cookout today? Good Christ. They were comin' out of the woodwork.

MARJORIE
And she has Tom.

LEO
What?

MARJORIE
The memory. His memory.

GERT
Yes.

MARJORIE
She has Tom's memory.

GERT
She's lucky.

LEO
(slow take to Gert)
What, you'd be happier if I was a memory?

PAT
We got grandkids too.

MARJORIE
Seattle. Too far.

LEO
There is no such thing.

GERT
(grunts)
Aah...

LEO
(mimics grunt)
"Aah" what?

GERT
Nothin'. Just "aah."

They all sit silently. Gert and Marjorie remain exhausted. Pat remains resigned to a life unknowing. Leo remains agitated, wondering what the hell is going on.

After a moment, Alma appears in the screen doorway. She stands there a second, holding the old hat box. She smiles at her friends. She opens the screen door, comes onto the porch, and takes her center seat between Gert and Marjorie. She places the box on her lap. Pat rises and goes to stand behind the ladies, looking at the box, as they are. Leo also rises, but stands to the side, taking the whole thing in.

Alma takes a deep breath, then opens the box. She takes out an old baseball mitt, slips the box to her side, and holds the mitt lovingly in her hands. Gert and Marjorie smile, and lean in to Gert. Pat is uncertain, but senses the warmth of the moment. Leo just can't take it anymore, and explodes.

LEO
You know, you're pissin' me off a little bit here, with the...she's got this and she's got that and oh, how lucky she is with the memory and the grandkids and there you are all... starin' God knows why at a baseball glove and I'm hearin' all this and I'm thinkin', you know, here I am...and here he is... and this is where we are...and that's where you are...and in a few minutes we'll be goin' home and they'll be goin' home and she'll be stayin' here that's where we'll all be. I mean, that's what I'm thinkin'. And that's what I'm sayin'...And all I'm sayin'...is...I'm wonderin'...if you know what you got.
         (directly, To Gert)
  That's all I'm sayin'. Do you know...what you got?

Leo stares defiantly at Gert. She stares back. Nobody moves. Gert holds the silence for as long as she can. Finally, she continues to look Leo directly in the eyes, and she sings:

GERT
"Only you can make the world seem right...

Pat takes his turn.

PAT

Only you...

GERT & PAT

...can make the darkness bright.

Marjorie rises and cuddles up to Pat, joining in as well. After a note or two, Alma rises and joins in too. They're surrounding the agitated Leo.

GERT & PAT & MARJORIE & ALMA

When you hold my hand I understand the magic that you do...

All look at Leo. He continues to smolder as his friends wait to see how he will react to the singing. Finally, he bursts into song, alone at first...

LEO

You're my dream come true...

ALL

My one and only...

Leo, now fully into the moment, in a very sweet falsetto, sings...

LEO

You!

ALL

One and only you!"

Leo contributes an elaborate Platters riff as the song ends.

<u>**ALL LIGHTS FADE TO BLACK**</u>

THE END

Made in the USA
Charleston, SC
05 November 2012